BEAUTIFUL HORSES

PORTRAITS

of

CHAMPION

BREEDS

BEAUTIFUL HORSES

PORTRAITS

of

CHAMPION
BREEDS

by LIZ WRIGHT
photographed by ANDREW PERRIS

Ivy Press

British Library Cataloguing in Publication Data
A catalogue record for this book is available from the British Library

This book was conceived, designed and produced by

Ivy Press
210 High Street, Lewes, East Sussex, BN7 2NS, UK

Creative Director **Peter Bridgewater**
Publisher **Susan Kelly**
Art Director **Wayne Blades**
Senior Editors **Jayne Ansell & Jacqui Sayers**
Designer **Ginny Zeal**
Photographer **Andrew Perris**
Illustrator **David Anstey**

ISBN: 978-1-78240-042-4
First Edition: 2013
Printed in China
Colour origination by Ivy Press Reprographics
Distributed worldwide (except North America) by Thames & Hudson Ltd.,
181A High Holborn, London WC1V 7QX, United Kingdom.

10 9 8 7 6 5 4 3 2

CONTENTS

INTRODUCTION

THE HORSE HAS PLAYED AN ENORMOUS PART IN human civilization and been an invaluable companion to us for thousands of years. From early man, who used the horse as a pack pony, to modern humans who developed it as a warhorse and were totally reliant on its strength as a workhorse, it is impossible to overestimate the importance of this animal in the development of human history. Although mechanization has now taken over many of the horse's traditional roles, it is still a crucial working animal in some areas.

As well as their more utilitarian uses, horses have long been popular for leisure and sport. Horse racing has been enjoyed for thousands of years and disciplines such as show jumping, eventing and dressage are also well established. New sports such as horseball are developing and gaining momentum. The diverse range of modern breeds means there is a horse perfectly suited to each discipline, from the diminutive SHETLAND pony – an excellent choice for fast obstacle (scurry) driving, to the THOROUGHBRED, whose breathtaking speed is much in demand for racing.

As diverse as horse breeds are, they all have one thing in common – they are all beautiful, with their own unique qualities. Championship shows celebrate the beauty and unique defining characteristics of each breed, with horses presented in the show ring for judging, having been painstakingly prepped for their moment in the limelight. Our photographer visited one such show to capture the stunning images in this book, revealing the spirit and elegance of each of the animals.

The photographs are accompanied by concise information on the defining characteristics of each breed, as well as its past and present place in human life, details of how it developed, and its relation to other breeds.

Origin and distribution information shows where each breed hails from, and how far it has now spread.

Above: The relationship between man and horse goes back thousands of years and is still going strong today.

The horses in this book come in all shapes, sizes and colours, but one thing is for sure – their owners all prize them. The uses of the horse may have changed over the centuries but its future seems in no doubt with so many people devoting their lives to the care and enjoyment of these beautiful animals.

HORSES IN CIVILIZATION

HUMANS HAVE HAD A VERY LONG ASSOCIATION with the horse. For 4,000 years, this animal has provided power and speed, and also has acted as a symbol of strength. The horse's earliest ancestor, Eohippus, which lived some 55 million years ago, was about the size of a modern-day hare, but over time evolved into the horse we know today.

It is thought that today's horses and ponies originated from three distinct types that were shaped by the different environments they evolved in. Cave paintings from around 2500BC have helped us understand what they looked like. The three types were the primitive Asiatic wild horse, known as the Steppe (still extant but mainly in captivity as the PRZEWALSKI horse); the slow, heavy breed type from northern Europe, known as the Forest; and the finer Tarpan from eastern Europe, also known as the Plateau.

It is thought the first horses were domesticated by nomads who used them not for riding, but for carrying goods and also for meat. Mesopotamia provides one of the first records of the use of horses in 2000BC, with

Above: Prehistoric rock paintings in the Bhimbetka caves, a World Heritage Site in India, show men out hunting on horseback.

records and paintings of chariots. The earliest horse breeders to have left records were the Assyrians, who bred horses strong enough to carry warriors clad in heavy armour, beginning the ongoing quest to breed bigger and stronger horses. By 2,500 years ago, the people of Persia were breeding horses that are thought to be the ancestors of today's ARAB horses.

Continuing the quest for greater size, the Forest breeds were used to produce heavyweight chargers for such peoples as the Goths who lived in modern-day northern and eastern Europe some 1,750 years ago. By the time of the Roman Empire, the use of horses for warfare, sport and draught was commonplace. As armies moved across countries and continents they brought their own types of horse with them, influencing local breeds.

As well as their uses in war, horses have played a crucial role in hunting, transport and agriculture through the centuries. The horse was at the peak of its popularity as a working farm animal in the early 1800s, but since mechanization it has carved out a new niche as a sports, leisure and companion animal.

THE DEVELOPMENT OF BREEDS

ONCE HUMANS STARTED TO HERD HORSES AND use them in combat, distinct breeds began to develop. A breed is essentially a response to a need – either the need of that horse to make the most of its surroundings, such as the hardy native ponies, or for man to refine the horse for his own uses, such as for strength, speed or for elegance. Although most breed standards are now set, breeds still develop as requirements for sport, leisure and companion animals change.

In the late 20th century there was a rise in the use of the 'warmblood' horse – developed by crossing carriage-type horses with THOROUGHBREDS to produce a formidable sports horse, displaying great athleticism, courage and stamina. Around the same time, the show pony stud book was established. The breed had started simply with native ponies being crossed with ARABS or small Thoroughbreds to produce children's riding ponies with impressive movement for the show ring. More recently, the coloured horses have been subdivided into types such as vanners and traditional gypsy cobs. Breeders are now also mating coloured horses to Thoroughbreds, to produce a coloured horse or pony that is athletic enough to compete in jumping and dressage at a high level.

Around the world there are many breeds of horse and pony that have adapted to cope with the terrain where they live, as well as the needs of the people. The FJORD pony, for example, is thought to have been in Norway since pre-Viking times. Ideally adapted to the mountainous habitat, it is also the perfect pack pony. The HANOVERIAN horse has a more modern history – it was the result of the foundation of a state stud in 1735 by George II, Elector of Hanover and King of England. He aimed to provide local people with good stallions and brought in HOLSTEINS, later introducing Thoroughbred blood to produce the athletic competition horse seen today.

The ultimate goal for breeders is to maintain traditional qualities, such as hardiness in natives, power in draught horses and endurance in Arabs, while meeting the demands of the modern market. Breed associations and horse shows reinforce these standards, encouraging only the best to breed.

Above: Equine evolution, breeding and crossing has resulted in the powerful, beautiful and graceful horses we know and love today.

BREED STANDARDS

BREED STANDARDS DEFINE THE CHARACTERISTICS of each breed. They act as a goal for breeders and help them to choose which animals to breed from to maintain the standards and improve their stock. They are usually set by breed associations and the older the breed, the longer the standards will have been in existence. They are not set by individuals, but by experienced breeders or show judges.

Breed standards reflect the appearance of the breed. For example: its height (the SHETLAND pony must not exceed 107 cm, or 10.2 hh); its head (the EXMOOR pony has large, wide-apart and prominent eyes with pale outlining); its colour (the HAFLINGER must have a flaxen mane and tail).

In more modern breeds, the breed standards will also reflect the purpose for which that breed was developed. The show hack, for example, is expected to show breathtaking elegance, whilst the MORGAN horse takes this a step further with a breed character statement: 'The beauty of the Morgan horse lifts the heart. The breed exists solely because it pleases people. It is their heritage.'

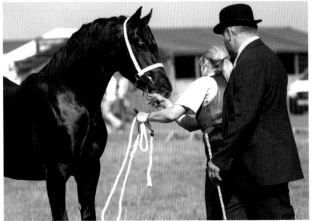

Above: Breed standards are set by breed associations and experienced judges are certified to judge one or several breeds.

If different breeds are judged alongside one another, for example in a mixed show class, they will be considered against their own breed standard, rather than in comparison to one another. Standards for a breed can also vary around the world, as breed societies in each country will set their own standards, although the country of origin will often issue an overall breed ideal.

Maintaining and, when necessary, revising breed standards is a huge responsibility. Decisions such as whether to increase the height of native ponies to reflect the better nutrition and demand for a bigger riding type must be weighed against possibly losing other characteristics that define it, such as its hardiness. These issues arise in every breed as the use of the horse changes. In the 20th century, horses went from having to hack miles to events to being transported by road – does this mean that stamina is no longer an issue? Only top class experts and breeders can decide, but the reality is that their decisions will impact far into the future. The show ring plays a very important part in this and essentially functions as a breeder's 'shop window'.

CHAMPIONSHIP SHOWS

PUT SIMPLY, THESE ARE PLACES WHERE OWNERS AND breeders come to show off their horses and ponies to their best advantage, in competition, to be judged by experts. With the rise of agricultural shows in the early 19th century, as a result of the agrarian revolution, the first show classes for working horses were established, celebrating the best of the breeds used for farm work and, later on, carriage work.

By the late 1800s more horse classes were added as the popularity of these shows grew, and prizes were also offered for hunters and hacks. In the 1930s classes for ponies were introduced and people increasingly began to recognize the value of their own native-bred animals. It wasn't really until the mid-1950s that showing really diversified into a wide range of classes, with new associations, such as the Ponies of Britain, setting a benchmark with their varied schedules and prestigious awards.

Championship shows never looked back in the UK, while around the world, bigger and better shows were increasingly taking place. German horse breeders and enthusiasts, for example, take

Above: This immaculately turned-out horse with its stunning dapple grey coat and braid forms a perfect partnership with its rider.

the performance of their horses very seriously. At the Equitana festival in Hengste, the Stallion Show sees leading warmblood and riding pony sires (established and future stallions) performing to an audience of 5,000 people. In the USA, state fairs include classes to accommodate all types of horses and riding. Around the world, classes have been added for new needs and breeds – many of which have been imported from other countries.

Championship shows set standards and competitors not only have to produce a horse that meets the criteria of its breed, but also one that is immaculately turned out and shows itself off to best advantage within the ring. Being trained to a high degree to do this is important for both the horse and its handler. As well as demonstrating obedience to its rider or handler, the horse must be unfazed by the crowds, lights and noise in the arena.

As well as the serious business of maintaining breed standards to their highest level, for owners and breeders, taking part in championship shows is also about having fun and sharing their passion with other like-minded people.

PREPARING FOR SHOWS

WEEKS OR EVEN MONTHS BEFORE A SHOW, breeders and owners must decide what to enter – horses will be appraised to identify the best ones, and then the preparation work begins in earnest to get each horse ready for its big appearance.

For an in-hand class (where the horses are not ridden, but led) the horse must be in tip-top condition and this cannot be achieved overnight. Weeks of optimal feeding, grooming and exercise are needed to turn a horse into a stunning show-winning superstar. Patient hours are spent in the schooling ring, training the horse to stand with all four legs in the correct position for its breed, to trot up on command and to walk in a relaxed and elegant manner – all of which will be required to pass the scrutiny of the judges. The handler, too, must learn to show the horse off, to believe that their exhibit is the best and show it with pride and skill. They must also be fit enough to run alongside the horse, to allow it to display its paces.

As the date of the show approaches, so the grooming regime intensifies. Headwear for the horse is selected in line with details set out in its breed standard – snowy white halters must be used for WELSH COB mares, intricate turn out is expected for the heavy horses, plain but scrupulously well-fitted and clean bridles are a must for the hunters, and glittering brow bands are required for the show ponies and hacks.

The day before a show every inch of the horse will be painstakingly washed. White legs are whitened to dazzling perfection, and white tails may be washed with special preparations to get them sparkling – each exhibitor will have their own way of achieving this. Rugs and sometimes hoods are used to keep the horse clean overnight, but there's also an emergency grooming kit to wipe off any grass stains or imperfections, and to add the finishing touches.

Above: The mane is a horse's crowning glory and a carefully plaited mane can visually lengthen or shorten a horse's neck.

Lotions may be used to enhance the outside of the eyes, show sheen and emphasize the glossiness of the coat. Some breeds must have their manes and tails plaited and the number of plaits can create the illusion of a longer or shorter neck. Finally, for big championship shows with a performance in the evening, glitter can be applied to reflect the lights for a true fairytale feel.

A JUDGE'S EYE VIEW

AT THE SHOW ITSELF, THE SHOWGROUND WILL BE arranged into rings, each of which will hold several classes throughout the day. Some rings may have jumps up for the working, hunter, pony or style classes, and others may have a dressage layout. Stewards will be allocated a ring and judges will have accepted classes to judge according to their area of expertise.

From the moment the judge steps into the ring, they must take charge of the class – and what they say goes. All classes are judged in a particular way, according to the requirements of the breed standards. The judges must know what to ask of competitors and what they expect, and also be an expert in the standards for the breeds they are judging. It is the competitor's job to present their horse in such a way that it can be properly judged – if a horse won't settle down or won't show a walk or a trot, the judge cannot evaluate it properly.

Exuberance and high spirits are allowed in some classes, such as those with young colts, but they must also show off their paces correctly and stand so that they can be considered.

In a typical in-hand class, the judge will begin by watching the horses walk around the ring, forming an initial opinion of the way in which they move and their type. They will examine each horse individually in order to determine how good an example of its breed or type it is. There will then be another chance for the judge to see how the horse performs as it is led away – to see if it is correct behind – and then trotted back again. This allows the judge to evaluate the movement of the horse from all angles. The judge may then walk around the line up once more, before placing the horses into their final order. The class ends with a glorious trot around the ring with the winners at the front.

Above: A red rosette is generally the ultimate prize in Britain but denotes second place in America, where blue is the winning colour.

In a ridden class, the emphasis is on the horse's obedience to the rider and its movement. A ridden hunter, will need to show all paces, but particularly a good gallop, while a child's pony must be well mannered. In harness classes, the horse must be responsive to the driver's instructions at all times.

Whichever class a horse is being shown in, it will be closely scrutinized by the expert eyes of the judge.

THE HORSES

This GORGEOUS GALLERY will put any amateur horse lover or expert *equiphile* through their paces. Don't canter too fast through our *harras of 40 horses*; each deserves close scrutiny. Judge for yourself as you put them through their paces – this is the MANE ATTRACTION.

SHIRE
GELDING

Known as both a gentle giant and a heavy draught horse, the SHIRE is thought to originate from the 'Great Horse' of medieval times that was developed to carry men in armour. Modern Shires are often seen in the show ring, either in harness or in hand, with manes and tails braided in the traditional way – originally a means of avoiding their hair becoming caught in the equipment they were pulling.

Features

Their feather (the long hair around the feet) is clean and combed for the show ring. Shires can be black, brown, bay or grey in colour – the dark colours coming from their European heritage. They weigh up to 1 tonne (0.98 tons).

Uses

Because of the Shire's size, strength and stamina, it has played a key part in heavy farm work and draught work in towns and cities. Shires could be seen pulling brewer's drays, coal wagons, hauling logs and loading at docks. A few working Shires still remain but most are shown at fairs and shows, providing a reminder of their part in our past.

Related Breeds

The Shire is thought to originate from crossing the 'Great Horse' with Flanders and Friesians from Europe. It is also related to the Clydesdale.

Size

Stallion ....167–178 cm
                    (16.2–17.2 hh)
Mare ....162–173 cm
                    (16–17 hh)

Origin & Distribution

As it was bred mainly in the shires of the Midlands and Cambridgeshire in the UK, it took the name of 'Shire' horse in 1884 having also been known as The Old English Cart Horse. It is widely distributed having been exported around the world.

England

MORGAN

MARE

This breed, now renowned for its beauty and elegance in the show ring, has its roots as an exceptionally hard-working farm horse. The original stallion, Justin Morgan, was very strongly built, winning various log-hauling contests. From these roots also came its kind nature. In 1961, the MORGAN was named the official state animal of Vermont and in 1970, the official state horse of Massachusetts, USA.

Features

This breed is noted for its compact size, alert, refined head and well-defined paces. Its coat can be black, bay, chestnut or brown. There are no white markings above the knee except on the face.

Uses

Morgans are part of American history, having been used in the military, on the farm and in harness. They declined in popularity in the early 1900s but today they are found in every discipline, from leisure riding, Western and English style, to dressage, show jumping and endurance. They are also found as stock horses and excel in driving.

Related Breeds

It is thought that the Morgan may have some relationship to the Thoroughbred and Arab and perhaps also some Dutch blood.

Size

Stallion ....144–158 cm
(14.1–15.2 hh)
Mare ....144–158 cm
(14.1–15.2 hh)

Origin & Distribution

Uniquely this breed descended from one stallion, Justin Morgan (named after his original owner). The breed thrives throughout the USA but is also found in Canada, the UK, throughout the rest of Europe, Australia and New Zealand.

USA

SUFFOLK

GELDING

The SUFFOLK (also known as the Suffolk Punch), was known for being economical to keep as it needed less feed than other working horses of a similar size. Its placid nature is cited as one of the reasons for its natural longevity. The Suffolk also matures comparatively early – going into work at around three years of age whereas other breeds may not be ready before the age of four or even five.

Features

All Suffolk horses are a rich chestnut in colour and their distinct conformation is of a large and powerful body set on short, sturdy legs, which have little or no feather. They can weigh up to 1 tonne (0.98 tons).

Uses

The Suffolk's good temperament, strength, early maturity, soundness (lack of lameness) and being economical to keep make it an ideal farm horse. The characteristic wide-set legs and lack of feather allowed them to work in crops without causing damage. They also worked on the roads hauling anything from farm produce to omnibuses.

Related Breeds

References to the Suffolk date back to the early 1500s. Although their origins are unknown, they are thought to be closer to the Haflinger than to other heavy horse breeds.

Size

Stallion ....163–171 cm
(16–16.3 hh)
Mare...............163–171 cm
(16–16.3 hh)

Origin & Distribution

As the name suggests, the breed originates from the county of Suffolk in England. It has been exported to Russia, North and South America, Australia, Africa and Europe but is on the rare breed list in the UK and the USA.

England

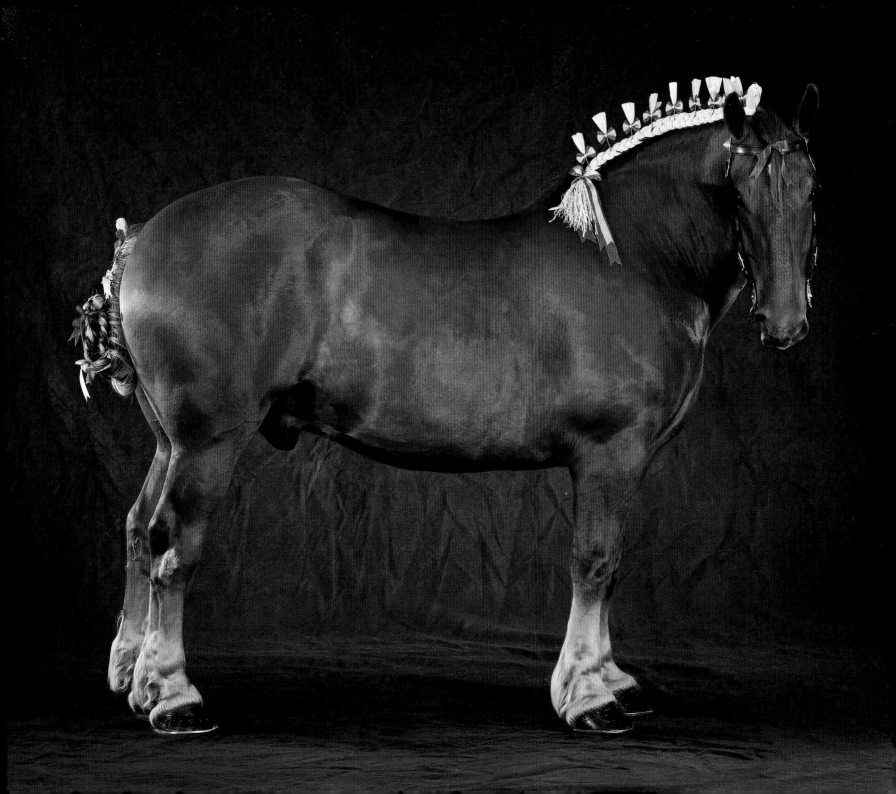

CONNEMARA

MARE

The CONNEMARA is known as an outstanding performance pony as its conformation and paces demonstrate. Strong and sound, the pony brings its working past to bear in its intelligence and willingness, while the influence of Spanish and Arab blood gives it courage and quality. A legend that it descended from horses that swam ashore from the Spanish Armada is not now thought to be true – trading is a more likely possibility.

Features

The well-sloped shoulders allow for free movement while the long, arched neck gives a good length of rein. Its coat is usually grey but can be dun, brown, bay, black and sometimes chestnut.

Uses

Developed along the western coast of Ireland, it was used in harness to carry seaweed. When it spread inland from the rocks of Connemara it gained a more nutritious diet and increased in size, but it retains its hardiness. It can be found in any sphere, from show jumping, junior eventing and pony club to dressage and driving, and is a sound and reliable riding pony.

Related Breeds

As well as the Spanish ancestry, it's thought Vikings brought ponies with them, so Scandinavian blood is part of the breed. In the early twentieth century, the breed was improved with Thoroughbred and Arab blood but now the stud book is closed.

Size

Stallion ....up to 148 cm
(14.2 hh)
Mare ....up to 148 cm
(14.2 hh)

Origin & Distribution

As the name suggests, this breed originated in Ireland in a remote and rocky area of County Galway. Now it can be found in the USA, Australia, New Zealand, Scandinavia and Europe.

Ireland

CLYDESDALE
MARE

The CLYDESDALE is a traditional Scottish farm and draught horse, known as an 'active' breed. This means it must show action when it moves – that is, when lifting the legs every shoe must be visible from behind. It has a reputation for outstanding limbs and feet and, despite it not being worked as hard as it once was, these are still important in the show ring, ensuring the future soundness of the breed.

Features

Short backed with an athletic body, the breed sports an arched neck and large, intelligent eyes. Its coat comes in bay, brown or black and there is often considerable white on the head and legs, which can run up to the body. A flash on the body is known as 'the Clydesdale mark'.

Uses

The soundness was put to good use with Clydesdales being a versatile farm horse, as happy in the plough as hauling heavy loads on rough terrain. This breed's kind, docile nature makes it ideal for working in pairs or as teams, which are able to haul prodigious weights.

Related Breeds

Shires were used in the second half of the nineteenth century to further develop the Clydesdale as a working horse. Originally bred for carrying rather than pulling, selective breeding and the introduction of Flemish blood developed its draught potential.

Size

Stallion ....175–183 cm
            (17.1–18 hh)
Mare ....170–178 cm
            (16.3–17.2 hh)

Origin & Distribution

This is a Scottish breed, originating in Lanarkshire. It was exported worldwide to North America, Australia, South America, Russia and throughout Europe.

Scotland

CLEVELAND BAY

GELDING

Although one of the oldest pure British breeds, the CLEVELAND BAY has achieved fame for its ability to cross with other breeds adding bone, size and stamina to lighter animals. Unfortunately, this caused the number of pure breed horses to fall dramatically but the breed is now valued again in its own right. The show ring has played a large part in its revival.

Features

As the name suggests, it is bay in colour with black points – meaning black legs, mane and tail. A small white star on the forehead is also allowed. It's well-built, with strong limbs and a deep body, giving it substance and stamina for riding and driving. Its large, fine ears are set on an intelligent-looking head.

Uses

A good, tough all rounder, the Cleveland Bay is able to carry heavier riders but can also perform in the hunting field and is renowned for its jumping ability. It is also an excellent harness horse – Queen Elizabeth II's husband Prince Philip uses teams of pure and part-breeds in competition as carriage horses. It is also one of the breeds of carriage horse in the Royal Mews in Britain.

Related Breeds

The Arab, Andulusian, Barb and Thoroughbred all played their part in developing the Cleveland as a quality coach horse. However, it is entirely distinctive from these breeds.

Size

Stallion ....162–168 cm
(16–16.2 hh)
Mare ....162–168 cm
(16–16.2 hh)

Origin & Distribution

Chiefly bred in Cleveland, north-east England, where it took its name. It was developed from an even older breed, the Chapman Pack Horse. Now it can be found in Europe, North America, Canada, South Africa, Asia and Australia.

England

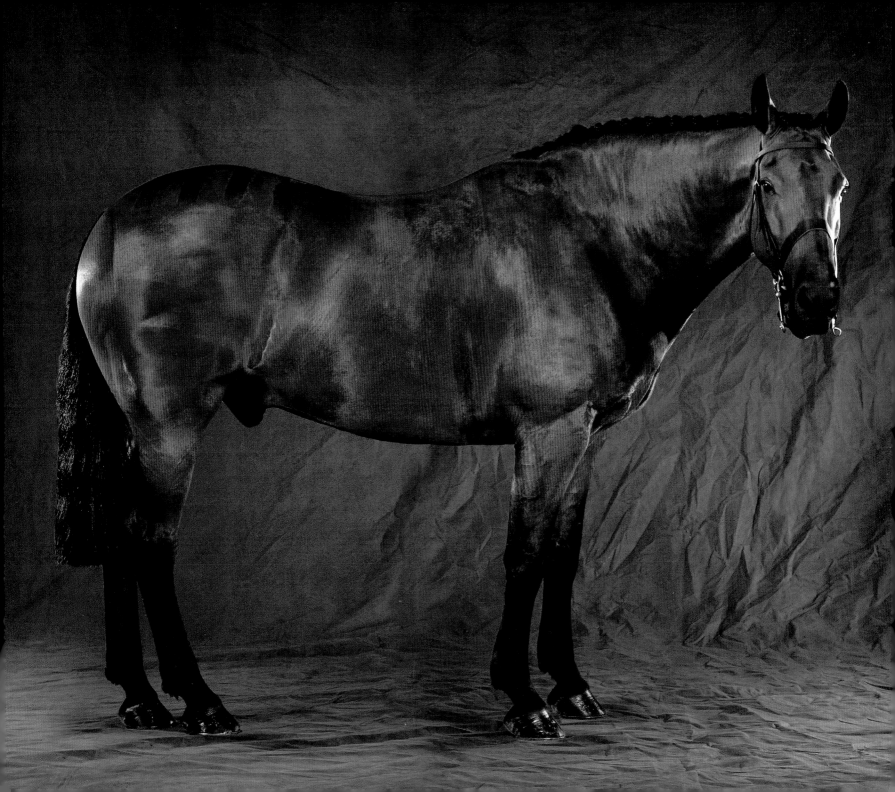

SHETLAND

MARE

The smallest of the British native breeds, the SHETLAND pony has a strength that belies its small size. It is also remarkably well adapted to the harsh environment of the northern Scottish islands that give it its name, and the low quality grazing found there. Even its movement, with the lift of the legs, reflects the rocky terrain it had to cover without stumbling.

Features

Hardiness, intelligence, small size and strength are the outstanding characteristics of this diminutive breed. It can be any colour except spotted. The Shetland gives the overall impression of toughness and vitality. Mane and tail should be long and full.

Uses

Today, the Shetland is traditionally a child's first pony and competes in both ridden and jumping breed classes, but recently the popularity of scurry driving has prompted much interest in its use as a harness pony. In the past, Shetland islanders used it as a pack pony carrying agricultural produce from field to croft to market. It was also used for work in coalmines.

Related Breeds

Due to its island home, it has remained quite pure but may share common ancestors with other European native ponies.

Size

Stallion ....up to 107 cm
(10.2 hh)
Mare ....up to 107 cm
(10.2 hh)

Origin & Distribution

Small ponies have been known in the Shetland Isles since the Bronze Ages. The Shetland may have originated from the Tundra pony and the Mountain type pony from southern Europe with an influx of blood from Norse visitors. It is found worldwide, including the Falkland Islands and Arctic Circle areas.

Scotland

NEW FOREST

GELDING

A versatile and good-natured pony, the NEW FOREST is the ultimate all-rounder. With quality from the various crossings made throughout its history, this pony is a hardy survivor that is well adapted to the challenges of living free in the forest. Its natural athleticism and adaptability mean that it is as happy in the show ring as show jumping and can be seen excelling in many spheres.

Features

Any colour except skewbald, piebald or blue-eyed cream. No white markings other than on the head and lower limbs. It has well-shaped hindquarters and a good depth of body with hard, round feet. The action is free and purposeful but without excessive knee action. The temperament is highly trainable.

Uses

An excellent riding pony for lightweight adults and children alike, the breed also performs well as a driving pony, bringing its surefootedness to both disciplines. In the show ring, it is usually shown with natural mane and tail, where it also jumps well and performs a good dressage test.

Related Breeds

Many influences have shaped the New Forest including the Thoroughbred, Arab and Hackney, which increased its size. Native breeds such as Exmoor, Dales and Dartmoor were used to maintain its pony characteristics.

Size

Stallion ....up to 148 cm
(14.2 hh)
Mare ....up to 148 cm
(14.2 hh)

Origin & Distribution

Wild ponies have lived in the New Forest in southern England for at least 900 years. The breed is now standardized with a stud book and has been exported to Europe, Scandinavia, North America, Australia and New Zealand.

England

DALES

STALLION

The DALES pony is the largest and heaviest British native breed. It truly earns its breed description as a strong, active pony, full of spirit. It has striking movement, with powerful hocks driving it forward to pick up the knees, yet the action is straight and purposeful. The body is compact and the head often has inward-curving ears and a broad forehead.

Features

With its profuse mane and tail, fine silky feather at the heel and distinctive active trot, it is an eye-catcher in the show ring. Its coat colour is mainly black, bay and brown and less commonly grey. However, it should not have excessive white markings.

Uses

The Dales can carry adults weighing up to 101 kg (16 st) as well as being a strong and reliable draught horse. Because of its good temperament and intelligence, it adapts well to other disciplines such as jumping and is a great long distance riding pony. In the past the Dales worked in lead mining, carrying heavy loads both underground and above ground. The British army used Dales ponies in both world wars.

Related Breeds

The Fell and the Dales share common ancestors. The Welsh Cob may have influenced the breed as shown in its action, and the Friesian and the Clydesdale may have also played a part.

Size

Stallion ....up to 148 cm
(14.2 hh)
Mare ....up to 148 cm
(14.2 hh)

Origin & Distribution

The Dales originates from the eastern side of the Pennine Hills in Yorkshire, UK and has been bred in northern England for many years. It can now be found in Europe, North America, Scandinavia and Australia.

England

APPALOOSA
GELDING

The APPALOOSA is most famous for the unique spotted pattern of its coat – hence it being commonly known as the 'spotty horse'. In addition to its markings, the breed also shares other characteristics such as good (and often striped) feet. The Appaloosa is the state horse of Idaho, USA.

Features

There are five main coat patterns. These are blanket – solid white area with a contrasting colour (possibly with spots) usually over the hip area; leopard – a white horse with dark spots all over the body; snowflake – a dark horse with white spots; frosted – a horse with some spotting over a blanket coat; and solid – solid colour showing other breed characteristics. It has some degree of pink and black mottled skin around the lips, muzzle, nostril or eye.

Uses

Very strongly branded as American, this breed is used in all forms of Western riding including gaited, where they are known as 'Walkaloosa'. Also used in endurance, jumping and dressage, but is a favourite in the show ring drawing an appreciative audience to see the variety of coat colours.

Related Breeds

Related to the Spotted Pony and Knabstrupper. Derived from Spanish horses left by the Spanish conquistadores in America, the spotted horses became a particular favourite of the Nez Perce Indian tribe of Idaho who practised selective breeding.

Size

Stallion ....148–158 cm
                (14.2–15.2 hh)
Mare ....148–158 cm
                (14.2–15.2 hh)

Origin & Distribution

The Appaloosa comes from the USA, particularly the area around Idaho, north-east Oregon and south-east Washington. It is now prized throughout the world with a British Association, European following and found in Australia and New Zealand.

USA

DARTMOOR

GELDING

The Dartmoor pony declined rapidly after the First World War. It now has rare breed status Britain, although it is a popular choice for exhibitors both in hand and under saddle as a child's pony. Hailing from the rugged moors of Dartmoor in the south-west of England, these ponies are very hardy yet they have an exceptionally kind temperament and are great fun to keep.

Features

With a distinctive small head of pony type and a face showing small alert ears, this appealing pony has small but hard, strong feet, a strong muscled body and a fairly high-set tail. Its colour is bay, brown, black, grey, chestnut or roan – excessive white markings are discouraged.

Uses

As the Dartmoor naturally has a good length of neck, it makes a safe child's riding pony as it gives the rider a feeling of safety as they have plenty of neck in front of them. It is also a good jumper and with its docile, willing nature it goes well in harness. In the past it worked as a pack pony and general farm help, and was used underground in mines.

Related Breeds

On the trade route between Exeter and Plymouth, horses such as Arabs and Barbs influenced the breed. It was also crossed with the Shetland to make smaller ponies for the mines but the stud book of 1899 standardized the breed.

Size

Stallion ....up to 122 cm
(12 hh)
Mare ....up to 122 cm
(12 hh)

Origin & Distribution

Dartmoor is in south-west England and ponies are thought to have lived there for thousands of years. They can now be found in mainland Europe, North America and Scandinavia.

England

THOROUGHBRED

GELDING

Legendary as the ultimate in equine performers, the THOROUGHBRED was first and foremost a racehorse. Speed and stamina combine with beauty to make the Thoroughbred in action a breathtaking sight that has entranced people for hundreds of years. Thoroughbreds are now also seen in the show ring as retrained racehorses, show hacks and riding horses, making this a very versatile breed.

Features

Any colour except multi-coloured, such as brown and white. They are classified as 'hot blooded', as they are bred for agility and performance, for which they need to show great courage and boldness.

Uses

Bred for flat and jump racing, the Thoroughbred has had a huge influence on other breeds when crossed to get quality or size. As horse sports such as eventing have developed, so the demand for Thoroughbred or 'near Thoroughbred' (horses with a lot of Thoroughbred blood in them) has increased. In the show ring, near Thoroughbreds dominate the hack classes.

Related Breeds

The British Show Hack, Riding Pony, Riding Horse and Hunter types all benefited from the infusion of Thoroughbred blood. The Anglo Arab is a Thoroughbred/Arab cross. Modern Warmbloods have Thoroughbred blood in varying degrees.

Size

Stallion ....152–168 cm
(15–16.2 hh)
Mare ....152–168 cm
(15–16.2 hh)

Origin & Distribution

All modern Thoroughbreds descend from three sires from the 1700s, which were used to improve the existing breed. All grey Thoroughbreds can be traced back to a single Arabian stallion. The Thoroughbred is distributed worldwide.

England

ARABIAN

MARE

The ARABIAN horse, or Arab, is believed to be the oldest and purest of horse breeds and the one that has had the most profound influence on other breeds. Many people believe this to be the most beautiful horse in the world. The Arabian has a true high spirit, with no nastiness of temperament. Its movement gives the impression of floating across the ground.

Features

The Arabian has a small 'dished' head, wide nostrils, prominent eyes and an impressive, floating action when it moves. Its coat is usually chestnut, bay, grey or black in colour.

Uses

Arguably the breed has been used largely to cross into other breeds, but its original use was to carry riders speedily, safely and with stamina across long tracts of desert. It was also used during wars, including the Crusades. Today it is valued for its beauty but it is a tough, sound breed that is still the ultimate endurance horse. In the show ring, these characteristics are valued and judged to maintain the breed. Arab horse racing has also seen a revival in recent years.

Related Breeds

These are too numerous to mention, but include the Thoroughbred, the Akhal Teke and the warmblood breeds. The Arab has been used to 'improve' some breeds of British show and native ponies, in particular, the Welsh.

Size

Stallion ....148–158 cm
(14.2–15.2 hh)
Mare ....148–158 cm
(14.2–15.2 hh)

Origin & Distribution

Ancient depictions in art show a horse very like the Arabian living in the Arabian Peninsula from around 2500BC. It has since spread worldwide.

Arabian peninsula

AMERICAN QUARTER HORSE

MARE

American settlers from Britain brought their love of racing with them and used the working horses of the time for quarter-mile straight sprint races. Through breeding, the hindquarters became more powerful and the chest broadened, allowing the AMERICAN QUARTER HORSE to move from a standstill to a flat-out gallop with remarkable ease. A real performer, many show classes are based around demonstrating this horse's speed.

Features

This breed has a compact but athletic frame, broad chest and powerful hindquarters. Its coat can be in any solid colour but not two colours, such as brown and white.

Uses

Its speed, stamina, intelligence and natural ability to anticipate the movements of cattle make this horse a real partner to a rancher. It's in great demand for leisure riding activities such as barrel racing and cattle cutting, and also is now racing again in its own classes. Also used for pleasure rides, its good manners and comfortable gaits make it excel in this field.

Related Breeds

It is descended from the Spanish breeds in America at the time of the first settlers and may have had Thoroughbred influence.

Size

Stallion ....150–163 cm
(14.3–16 hh)
Mare ....150–163 cm
(14.3–16 hh)

Origin & Distribution

The first settlers on the East Coast found only a few horses, quite inbred, left by the Spanish conquistadores many years previously. The breed today is found worldwide, especially in regions with ranging cattle, such as Africa and Australia.

USA

HIGHLAND

MARE

There are two distinct types of HIGHLAND pony, though only one breed standard – the larger mainland type and the smaller and lighter Western Isles type. It is an outstandingly sturdy pony with an inquisitive and intelligent nature. The appearance gives an impression of strength but keeps the true pony type. The colours are striking, with silver manes and tails often being a feature.

Features

The Highland is a deep-bodied, substantial pony. Various shades of dun make this a distinctive pony but it also can be grey, brown, black, chestnut with silvery mane and tail, and brown.

Uses

This breed is still used in its native Scotland to carry stags from deer shooting. Used as a mount in the First World War and Boer War, its other functions have included being a shepherd's pony and a farm horse. Today it is a good weight-carrying riding pony, able to manage an adult, but also kind enough for a child. It's still used for pulling, especially in woodland work where it does less damage to the ground than a vehicle.

Related Breeds

Many breeds have influenced the Highland's modern characteristics including, it is thought, the Clydesdale and Arab. It's likely that it was also influenced by the Percheron and the Dales pony.

Size

Stallion ....132–148 cm
          (13–14.2 hh)
Mare ....132–148 cm
          (13–14.2 hh)

Origin & Distribution

Originating from the Highlands and islands off the west coast of Scotland, this breed is thought to have developed from the northern European horse originally. Found in Europe, Sweden, North America, Australia and New Zealand.

Scotland

LIGHTWEIGHT COB

MARE

The Cob, as a description of a type of horse, has been in existence for hundreds of years and is associated with thick-legged, stocky horses capable of carrying weight or of working on the farm. The modern Cob has not changed dramatically, but it has been subdivided into the categories of lightweight cob; heavyweight cob and maxi cob. These classifications are based on the horse's height as well as the weight it can carry.

Features

The Lightweight Cob has strong, stocky legs. Powerful hindquarters are a feature of the type, but the head, although sensible, should show intelligence and a full kind eye. In the show ring it should be able to carry up to 89 kg (14 stone).

Uses

The Cob was a versatile animal doing everything from farm work to pulling the market cart, and taking the family on outings. It was valued as a hunter and more than played its part in the war years. Today the Lightweight Cob is a show type but also jumps well and is an ideal leisure horse.

Related Breeds

A cob is a type and can be formed of almost any breed except such breeds as Arab or Thoroughbred. Likely breeds to create a cob are native ponies, traditional cobs and draught horses.

Size

Stallion ....148–155 cm
　　　　　　　(14.2–15.1 hh)
Mare ....148–155 cm
　　　　　　　(14.2–15.1 hh)

Origin & Distribution

The cob type is descended from the coldblooded draught horses of northern Europe and it was used on farms throughout this region. It is now widely distributed and seen not only in the show ring but on farms and smallholdings in areas where people still rely on horse power.

Northern Europe

NATIVE COLOURED
GELDING

This active horse or pony is distinctive for being two or three coloured, including white. The NATIVE COLOURED is always shown with an unbraided mane and tail and although trimmed, it retains its natural features. As the coloured pony and horse became more popular in the show ring in the 1980s, societies and associations subdivided the groups to make it easier to have consistent standards.

Features

They are derived from native ponies worldwide so are hardy with a purposeful movement. The feather on the legs must not start from the hock or back of the knee, unlike the traditional Coloured Cob. Feather is variable in amount but never comes more than 2.5 cm (1 in) down the hoof. They can be any height.

Uses

With such a range of heights, the Native Coloured can be seen in almost all equine spheres from leisure and pleasure riding to show jumping and cross country, Western riding, driving and as an eye-catching horse or pony in the show ring. It enjoys horse agility competitions and is always a strong and useful pony.

Related Breeds

Any native breed can be a cross for these ponies although they do not have to show native pony blood as they are a type within the coloured standards. Origin does not have to be known.

Size

Pony ....up to 148 cm
(14.2 hh)
Horse ....over 148 cm
(14.2 hh)

Any height but subdivided for the purposes of showing between pony and horse.

Origin & Distribution

The Native Coloured is identified as a recognizable type by the relevant societies. Countries worldwide have their own variation on this pony.

Northern Europe

RESCUE HORSE

GELDING

Horses and ponies worldwide can be mistreated, but thanks to equine welfare groups, charities and private individuals, some of them are rescued and rehabilitated. A RESCUE HORSE can be any type as unfortunately no breed is immune to mismanagement. Rescue horses can be very rewarding animals and are often taken to shows by their rescuers.

Features

Horses and ponies can be rescued at any age from a wide variety of situations, from direct cruelty to neglect. Some are given up by owners who can no longer afford them, while others are the subject of court cases. Some are trained, while others may be completely unhandled. The task is to reintroduce them to normal equine life and find them a good home.

Uses

Rescue horses and ponies have many uses, from being kept as companion animals for other horses or ponies, to competing at top shows. The horse pictured was rescued as part of a cruelty case, but having been successfully rehabilitated he is now very successful in the traditional coloured classes.

Related Breeds

All breeds and types can become a 'rescued horse' through no fault of their own. Owners' circumstances change and ignorance can lead to inadvertent cruelty.

Size

Pony ....up to 148 cm
(14.2 hh)
Horse ....over 148 cm
(14.2 hh)
Rescue horses and ponies can be any size.

Origin & Distribution

Rescued horses and ponies are in every country in the world. They are normally gelded by their rescuers to help prevent more unwanted horses and ponies being bred.

Globally

NORWEGIAN FJORD

GELDING

Unchanged for hundreds of years, the NORWEGIAN FJORD is a powerful dun pony that is instantly recognizable with its distinctive colour and physique. The mane is usually clipped to about 10 cm (4 inches) in length, making it stand upright and highlighting the black that is often found hidden within the light-coloured hair.

Features

Their long and pure-bred ancestry means these ponies often have primitive marks on them, such as a dark dorsal stripe down their back and 'zebra' markings on the lower legs. Short, strong legs support a deep body and the head is broad with small ears. Hard, sound feet are also a feature.

Uses

Although there are runestone carvings in Norway showing them used for the Viking's favourite sport of pony fighting, Norwegian Fjord ponies actually have a very calm temperament. They were and still are used for draught work on the small farms in the fjords, being ideal for logging and in harness. Today they are also sought after for adult and younger riders and can be driven as matched teams.

Related Breeds

In the remote and mountainous parts of Norway, these ponies did not have many visitors to facilitate interbreeding. There is speculation that heavy draught breeds such as the Suffolk horse may be related.

Size

Stallion ....135–150 cm
(13.1–14.3 hh)
Mare ....135–150 cm
(13.1–14.3 hh)

Origin & Distribution

Arguably one of the oldest and purest breeds of pony, dating back to at least the Vikings, they are bred in much of Norway. They are now popular worldwide and can be found in the UK, Europe, USA, Canada, Australia and New Zealand.

Norway

BRITISH WARMBLOOD
MARE

The British Warmblood Society was formed in 1977 in response to the need to breed the BRITISH WARMBLOOD – a type of horse that would excel in the highest of competitive disciplines such as top-class dressage, eventing and show jumping. The aim was to produce horses able to compete at international level in all of these highly challenging disciplines.

Features

As they are a type rather than a breed their basic criteria is enhanced based on performance, competition record and conformation as well as having a stud book recording the bloodlines. Stallions and breeding mares are closely scrutinized. To meet the demands of the sport, they must be athletic and are normally strong with a willing temperament.

Uses

They are well known for excelling in dressage at the highest level as their conformation and breeding allow them to move in a free and 'elevated' way. They reach the very top in show jumping and are popular for all levels of eventing. Their athleticism and temperament make them a perfect leisure ride.

Related Breeds

Warmbloods are a combination of hot-blooded equines such as the Arab and Thoroughbred, and coldblooded, which are mostly draught breeds. German warmblood horses are very influential in the British Warmblood.

Size

Stallion ....158–178 cm
             (15.2–17.2 hh)
Mare ....158–178 cm
             (15.2–17.2 hh)

Origin & Distribution

Since the increased interest in the warmblood during the 1970s, it has spread quickly worldwide as its top-level sporting abilities were realized; warmbloods from all countries are well represented at the Olympics.

UK

FRIESIAN

GELDING

One of the oldest breeds of horse in the world, the FRIESIAN is a proud-looking horse with an arched neck showing off a flowing mane. It was crossed with horses of the Crusades, and later Spanish horses, to lighten the breed, but it was also used to create weight-carrying warhorses. The colour is always black and the only white allowed is a small white star.

Features

The longish head with its typically short ears and intelligent expression is set high upon a compact and powerful body. The strong limbs have plenty of 'bone' (are sturdy in appearance) and the silky feathering is always left untrimmed. The trot is high stepping and speedy. The impression is of eye-catching power.

Uses

The Friesian was a draught horse that worked on farms and even became popular for trotting races, although it nearly died out before enjoying a revival in the mid-twentieth century. It is very powerful but has a calm nature, so is widely used for private and commercial driving and is often used for funerals. It's also a capable and exciting ride and a good all-rounder.

Related Breeds

As it's been around so long, the Friesian has influenced many breeds but the ones that are acknowledged include the Shire, Fell, Dales, Welsh Cob and Oldenburg.

Size

Stallion ....153–163 cm (15–16 hh)

Mare ....153–163 cm (15–16 hh)

Origin & Distribution

Bones of a horse of this type have been found in Friesland in the Netherlands and it's thought it was descended from a heavy, coldblooded horse that survived the Ice Age. Now found throughout Europe, the UK, North America, Canada, Australia and New Zealand.

HAFLINGER
GELDING

Instantly recognizable, the HAFLINGER is a very distinctive type with a flowing flaxen mane and tail, and powerful body. A true working pony, this is a very sound animal and is renowned for its long life – said to be able to work into its thirties. It is named after the village of Hafling in the Austrian mountains, where it remained quite isolated, although the breed has now been standardized.

Features

A true pony, short, powerful legs support a deep, strong body. Yet they have a very active movement due to their powerful hindquarters. The head has a broad forehead, large intelligent eyes and small ears. The uniform colour of chestnut also allows for white markings on the face and legs.

Uses

The Haflinger was initially used as a pack pony and for general farm work on steep mountain slopes. Now this versatile pony is in demand for leisure riding for both children and adults. It's also an active but sensible driving pony whose colours match well and it has a strong presence in the show ring.

Related Breeds

The Haflinger is likely to be of a similar genetic pool to the Norwegian Fjord and some northern European native ponies. It also has genetic similarities to the Suffolk.

Size

Stallion ....138–148 cm
          (13.2–14.2 hh)
Mare ....138–148 cm
          (13.2–14.2 hh)

Origin & Distribution

The Haflinger's origins are hardy Austrian mountain ponies but it was improved with Arab blood in the nineteenth century. After the Second World War, it became popular in Europe, the UK, North America and more recently in Australia and New Zealand.

Austria

WELSH MOUNTAIN PONY

STALLION

Enthusiasts argue that the WELSH MOUNTAIN PONY, or Welsh Section A, is the most beautiful breed of native pony. With its large eyes, small ears, broad forehead and tapering muzzle, it is easy to see why. Add to that its impressive action and character and this pony exudes star quality. Some still run semi-feral in Wales, helping maintain the hardiness of the pony.

Features

Any solid colour is permitted; often grey but also seen as palomino, chestnut (often with flaxen mane and tail) and bay. White markings on the face and legs are accepted. It has a very active trot, which is encouraged in the show ring. Strong, short limbs support a deep but athletic body.

Uses

The extreme hardiness of this breed and its surefootedness made it a perfect companion for shepherds and it was strong enough to carry a small adult. Today it is a star in the show ring both under saddle and in hand. An all-round children's pony with a good jump, it also excels in harness both for performance classes and for show.

Related Breeds

It's thought that Eastern breeds, such as the Arab, brought to the UK by the Romans influenced these native mountain ponies. The Welsh Mountain has since been used to develop the British Riding pony and has also influenced the Pony of the Americas and the Australian pony.

Size

Stallion ....122–127 cm
(12–12.2 hh)
Mare ....122–127 cm
(12–12.2 hh)

Origin & Distribution

As the name suggests, the home of the Welsh Mountain Pony is Wales, but it is now truly worldwide in distribution.

Wales

COLOURED COB
GELDING

The striking COLOURED COB originated as a Romany gypsy pony and its strong body and legs were needed to pull large covered caravans. Its calm temperament reflects that it lived close to the family and was often ridden and cared for by children. The Cob's finely tuned body moves with a purposeful trot.

Features

They are often bi-coloured – brown, black or chestnut and white – and in their natural state have abundant manes and tails and huge amounts of feather. In the show ring they are displayed traditionally with full mane, tail and feathers or 'hogged and trimmed' meaning the mane is shaved off and feathers are trimmed back to the legs (as shown).

Uses

The gentle 'can-do' temperament of the Coloured Cob, coupled with its strength, has meant that it has spread from the travelling community to a wider world where it is valued as a riding animal in all disciplines. Still also valued as a harness animal, it is a great all-rounder and has its own range of show classes and societies.

Related Breeds

No one knows how the Romany gypsies bred these ponies but it is suspected that Shires, Clydesdale, Dales and Fell were included and more recently the Welsh Cob.

Size

Pony .... up to 148 cm
(14.2 hh)
Horse .... over 148 cm
(14.2 hh)

Any height but subdivided for the purposes of showing between pony and horse.

Origin & Distribution

These ponies are valued worldwide and are found throughout mainland Europe, the UK, North America, Canada, Australia and New Zealand.

Northern Europe

TRADITIONAL COLOURED COB
GELDING

Recognizable for its bold two-coloured coat and abundance of hair, the TRADITIONAL COLOURED COB was originally developed by Romany gypsies to pull their caravans and live alongside their family. During the First World War horses could be requisitioned by armies, but two-coloured horses were exempt from this as they were felt to be too visible on the battlefield. As a result, breeding these cobs became more popular as they would not be taken.

Features

Traditional Coloured Cobs are either black, brown, or chestnut and white. In their natural untrimmed state they have very full manes — sometimes almost reaching the ground — full tails and huge amounts of feathering around the foot. In the show ring they can be shown in full traditional beauty or fully trimmed up.

Uses

This breed is a good all-rounder with a willing temperament but is most often seen in harness or in the show ring where the silky feathers and mane are groomed to glossy perfection to show off their unique appearance.

Related Breeds

The Romany gypsies did not keep records of breeding but it is thought that the Shire, Clydesdale, Dales and Fell were all included and, more recently, the Welsh Cob has also been used.

Size

Pony ....up to 148 cm
               (14.2 hh)
Horse ....over 148 cm
               (14.2 hh)

Any height but subdivided for the purposes of showing between pony and horse.

Origin & Distribution

This breed has been in existence since Medieval times. Now these ponies are valued throughout Europe, the UK, North America, Canada, Australia and New Zealand.

Northern Europe

WELSH PONY
MARE

An elegant and useful riding pony for children, the WELSH PONY is also referred to as the Welsh pony of riding type, and the Welsh Section B. While retaining the distinctive pony type, infusions of Arab and Polo Pony blood have increased the size and refined the frame to produce this athletic performer. The Welsh Pony was 'improved' to meet increasing demand for children's ponies in the late 1960s.

Features

Any solid colour is permitted and white markings on the face and legs are accepted. It has a trot that appears to 'float', giving the impression of free flowing movement. A very well defined, small head is placed on a relatively long neck, and a short back, broad chest and sloping shoulder add to its athletic ability.

Uses

The Welsh Pony is an impressive performer that is often seen in competitive jumping and junior dressage. It's a great pony club pony as it is extremely versatile. In the show ring its movement and elegance make it a natural performer both in hand and under saddle. It's also a stylish but useful driving pony.

Related Breeds

The Welsh Pony was developed from the Welsh Mountain Pony using Arab, Thoroughbred and Polo Pony blood, but now it is standardized. It played a fundamental part in the formation of the British Riding Pony and has also influenced the Pony of the Americas and the Welara pony.

Size

Stallion ....up to 138 cm
(13.2 hh)
Mare ....up to 138 cm
(13.2 hh)

Origin & Distribution

The original Welsh Pony was a shepherd's pony. The 'improved' pony still has a huge following in its native Wales but is now distributed worldwide.

Wales

SHETLAND

STALLION

Hardy and small in stature, the SHETLAND pony is enormously strong for its size. Living naturally in the wild, harsh environment of the Shetland Isles to the north of Scotland, this pony had to adapt to severe conditions to survive, yet it has become a much-loved child's pony all over the world.

Features

Any colour except spotted is allowed so the bi-colours such as brown and white are accepted. It has short, strong legs and a round body with profuse mane and tail and small ears. It moves straight and true, and is very sure-footed – as it has to be in its native terrain.

Uses

In the past the Shetland pony played a vital role in crofting. It was also essential for bringing in peat. Later on, its small size made it a popular choice for work below ground in coalmines in the UK and further afield. Now it is known as a child's first pony, on and off the lead rein, and competes in its own breed classes. It's also much in demand as a harness pony, especially for driving around a timed obstacle course in scurry driving.

Related Breeds

In its far-flung island home, the Shetland remained isolated from other influences but is thought to share similar ancestors to other northern European ponies.

Size

Stallion ....up to 107 cm
(10.2 hh)
Mare ....up to 107 cm
(10.2 hh)

Origin & Distribution

Small ponies have been on the Shetland Isles since the Bronze Ages. It is thought that it may have originated from the Tundra pony and the Mountain type pony from southern Europe, with an influx of blood from Norse visitors. It is now found worldwide, including the Falkland Islands and Arctic Circle areas.

Scotland

FIRST RIDDEN RIDING PONY
MARE

The FIRST RIDDEN RIDING PONY, also known as a 'show pony', is very attractive with elegant limbs, long stride and a pretty head. These ponies are also classified under the umbrella of 'British Riding Pony'. The First Ridden type is aimed at children up to ten years old, after they have come off the lead rein and before they go into the bigger show pony classes.

Features

Although the pony must have excellent manners and be within the capabilities of the child, it must also be elegant and eye-catching. This pony is shown with a plaited mane and tail and a colourful browband, which often matches the rider's ribbons and buttonhole. The overall picture is one of charm and grace, coupled with the pony's gentle nature.

Uses

The increasing popularity of horse shows from the 1920s onwards created demand for a special type of children's riding pony. The First Ridden was developed for the show ring and can also be shown in hand. It can also be seen at pony clubs, taking part in junior dressage and some are very keen jumpers.

Related Breeds

The Riding Pony was developed using native ponies such as the Welsh and Dartmoor, as well as Polo Ponies, small Thoroughbreds and Arabs.

Size

Stallion 122–148cm
(12–14.2 hh)
Mare...............122–148cm
(12–14.2 hh)

Origin & Distribution

Early riding ponies were first crosses, but the British Riding Pony now has its own stud book and is a recognized show pony. Countries such as the USA have also followed suit by developing a lighter and more elegant child's pony.

UK

WELSH COB
STALLION

The WELSH COB, or Welsh Section D, is a powerful, compact pony with the biggest trot of all ponies – and arguably horses. Its high knee action is balanced by a hind leg capable of maximum flexion, propelling it across the ground at speed. A life-sized statue of a Welsh Cob stallion was erected in the town of Aberaeron, Wales in 2005 in recognition of the importance of this horse to the area.

Features

Any solid colour is permitted. White markings on the face and legs are accepted – white stockings are valued in the show ring as they highlight the movement. It has short, powerful legs and large hindquarters. It is powerfully built and has huge resources of stamina. The quality pony head is set high on the body.

Uses

Originally a farmer's pony, the Welsh Cob was the workhorse of the small farm, but also took part in trotting races. Today it is a great pony for adult riders as it can carry weight and provide an exciting ride. It also jumps well. It has a unique place as a harness pony where its action and strength come fully into play.

Related Breeds

The Welsh Cob is likely to be genetically similar to the Fell and Dales and has Arab and eastern influence.

Size

Stallion ....over 137.2 cm
(13.2 hh)
Mare ....over 137.2 cm
(13.2 hh)

Origin & Distribution

The Welsh Cob originates from the west coast of Wales where a number of famous Welsh Cob studs are situated. Welsh Cobs are worldwide in their distribution.

Wales

HANOVERIAN
MARE

One of the first warmblood horses to be established, following the inheritance of the British throne by the Elector of Hanover, George II in the eighteenth century, the HANOVERIAN has since influenced other warmblood types including the British Warmblood. Developed to be a dual-purpose farm and riding horse, increasing amounts of Thoroughbred blood have turned it into a superstar sports horse.

Features

Outstanding conformation coupled with athletic ability make this a refined looking horse with a strong, deep body, sloping shoulders and a quality, medium-sized head. It is found in all solid colours but especially in chestnut and bay. For the show ring the mane is plaited, and the tail either plaited or trimmed.

Uses

Hanoverians have racked up an impressive number of Olympic medals in dressage and show jumping and also excel in eventing. In the USA, they also enjoy success in the show hunter class. They are bred to compete at top level but are enjoyed by many people at all levels.

Related Breeds

Originally developed from the Spanish, Andalusian and Holstein, and crossed with the carriage horses of the eighteenth century, the breed had Thoroughbred and Trakehner re-introduced after the Second World War.

Size

Stallion ....158–171 cm
            (15.2–16.3 hh)
Mare ....158–171 cm
            (15.2–16.3 hh)

Origin & Distribution

The Hanoverian originated when George II founded the stallion depot at Celle using Holstein and English Thoroughbreds in 1735. Today the Hanoverian is found worldwide.

Germany

MINIATURE HORSE
STALLION

The one characteristic that all of the different types of MINIATURE HORSE have in common is their diminutive size. Despite being very small, they are known as miniature horses rather than ponies as their proportions and conformation are closer to that of a horse. Different types of miniature horse were developed in Europe and South America, but there are now dedicated societies around the world that support the breeding and showing of these tiny horses.

Features

Bearing out its different origins, the Miniature Horse comes in various types, from the stockier animal to a finer type. It also comes in the widest range of coat colours, with all colours being allowed. They need to be alert but calm in disposition as they are often kept as pets.

Uses

In the mid 1800s, some were used in northern Europe as pit ponies. Now they are sometimes used to pull small carriages, and increasingly play a part in pet therapy – with trained animals being taken on therapeutic visits to help sick people.

Related Breeds

Many breeds have influenced the different types, including the Shetland, Dartmoor, Pony of the Americas, Hackney, and particularly the Falabella miniature horse from Argentina.

Size

Stallion ....under 86–97 cm
(8.2–9.2 hh)
Mare ....under 86–97 cm
(8.2–9.2 hh)

Origin & Distribution

Miniature horses were first bred in about 1650 as pets for Europe's Hapsburg royal family. The Falabella, a distinct breed of miniature horse, was later developed in Argentina. Today the USA has led the way in refining the type, but now it is popular in the UK, mainland Europe, Australia and New Zealand.

Argentina

Northern Europe

RIDING HORSE
GELDING

Although all horses can be ridden, the RIDING HORSE is defined as a distinct type for the show ring. This not only covers its conformation but also extends to the way in which it performs, its manners and its obedience while under saddle. The desire for a quality riding horse to provide comfortable transport as well as elegance is nothing new, but this type of horse was standardized or the show ring in the second half of the twentieth century.

Features

This type needs to have substance to be able to carry an average weight adult, to have a sparkle about it but no skittishness and it needs to move freely and with long, swinging strides. It is bred to have correct conformation and move well.

Uses

The Riding Horse can be shown in hand, ridden or sidesaddle. It is always beautifully turned out for the show ring and is allowed to wear a very decorated brow band. It is shown plaited and trimmed. It is also a lovely leisure horse for hacking, hunting, jumping and competing in dressage and horse trials.

Related Breeds

Riding Horses are greatly influenced by Thoroughbreds. Their substance often comes from larger native breeds such as the Connemara.

Size

Subdivided:
Small ....148–158 cm
             (14.2–15.2 hh)
Large ....over 158 cm
             (15.2 hh)

Origin & Distribution

The Riding Horse was developed as a type during the twentieth century. It is now mainly found in Europe, North America, Australia, New Zealand and South Africa.

UK

BRITISH RIDING PONY

MARE

The BRITISH RIDING PONY is a very specific type of pony, sometimes referred to as a show pony, reflecting its flamboyance, extravagant action and pretty head. Despite its exuberance and star quality, it also has to show exemplary manners to be suitable for children to ride. It was developed to meet an increasing demand for a quality pony for children for the show ring in the 1920s and 1930s.

Features

This pony should catch the eye with its elegance and star quality. Its sloping shoulder allows for free flowing leg action carrying a compact body with a broad chest. The exquisite head is set high on a good length of neck.

Uses

This is a pony for the show ring that is capable of a fabulous display under saddle when ridden by a child. It is shown fully plaited with the tail either plaited or trimmed and the bridle will have a colourful brow band. It can also be shown in hand by an adult. Out of the show ring, its pony background means it can become a fast, keen jumper and can excel in junior dressage.

Related Breeds

Native ponies, in particular the Welsh and to an extent the Dartmoor, were the foundation of the British Riding Pony and these breeds were crossed with small Thoroughbreds and Arabs including Polo Ponies.

Size

Subdivided into three sections:
up to 127 cm (12.2 hh)
127–138 cm (12.2–13.2 hh)
138–148 cm (13.2–14.2 hh)

Origin & Distribution

Originally developed from the native pony, the British Riding pony is now a type with its own stud book and has been exported worldwide.

UK

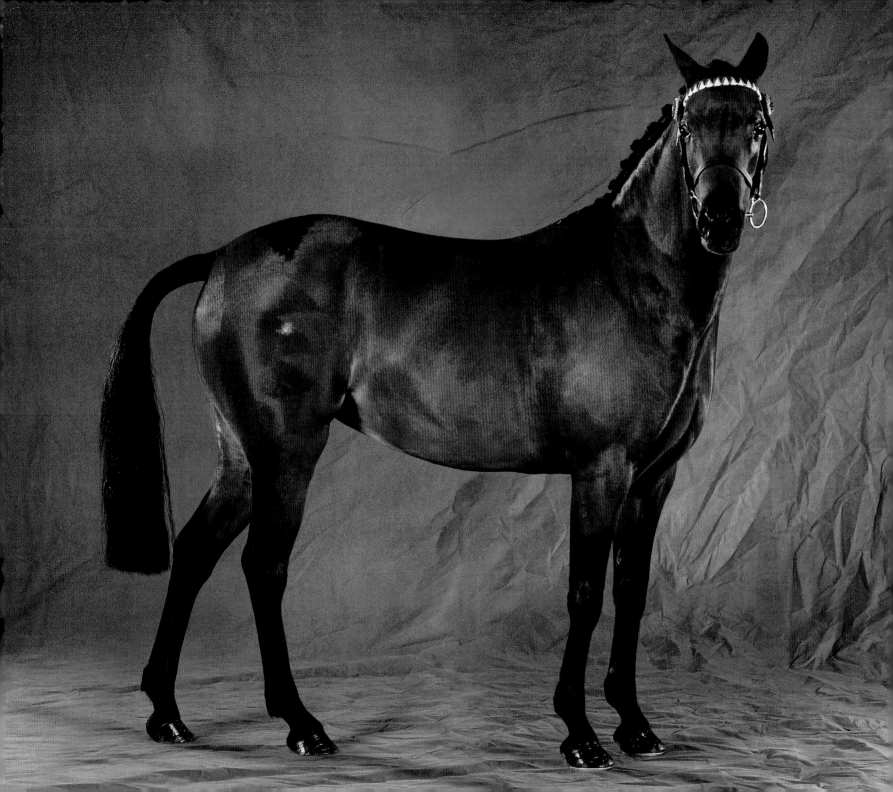

WELSH COB

GELDING

Known for its fabulously high stepping, powerful and ground-covering trot, the WELSH COB, or Welsh Section D, is instantly recognizable with its typically pony head, small alert ears and large generous eyes. The overall impression is one of controlled power mingled with spirit and strength. It is breathtaking in the show ring when shown performing its famous extended trot.

Features

Often in strong, solid colours such as black or chestnut, any solid colour is permitted. The white legs are sought after in the show ring as they highlight the extravagant action. Powerful hindquarters are coupled with hocks that flex to drive forward the short, strong limbs and allow the Welsh Cob to flamboyantly cover ground. Manes and tails are mostly left free.

Uses

Trotting races as well as work on the farm was the job of the Welsh Cob not so long ago. But now its strength and versatility plus its hardiness make it a sought after pony for adults of all sizes for riding, jumping and hunting. In harness it excels due to its movement and its physical stamina and strength.

Related Breeds

The Welsh Cob is likely to be genetically similar to the Fell and Dales and has Arab and eastern influence. It is also related to the now extinct Norfolk Roadster.

Size

Stallion ....over 137.2 cm
(13.2 hh)
Mare ....over 137.2 cm
(13.2 hh)

Origin & Distribution

Welsh Cob country is along the west coast of Wales, but it was also noted in Cardiganshire, Pembrokeshire and other areas of Wales. Today, Welsh Cobs are distributed worldwide.

Wales

IRISH DRAUGHT

MARE

Famous worldwide for its stamina, jumping ability and its soundness of limb and temperament, this active, clean-legged horse commands respect. Crossed with other draught horses to produce a farm horse, the IRISH DRAUGHT horse is now a standardized breed. Ireland (and Britain's) love of hunting ensured this breed's popularity, but it is now increasingly seen in the show ring, both under saddle and in hand.

Features

The strong body, broad chest and powerful hindquarters are set on strong limbs with no feather. The head is handsome and gives the impression of intelligence. The action should be free and smooth but without excessive knee movement. Its coat comes in all solid colours, including grey.

Uses

The Irish Draught horse was originally part of Irish farming life as a light draught horse. It was developed for hunting and then became a popular cross for top-class show jumpers. It's an excellent all-rounder and up to carrying a substantial adult.

Related Breeds

Indigenous Irish breeds coupled with Spanish blood were the foundation for this horse, but Clydesdale and other draught horses were also introduced. Thoroughbreds were used to refine the breed – this mare is an example of a Thoroughbred cross.

Size

Stallion ....160–170 cm
(15.3–16.3 hh)
Mare...............155–165 cm
(15.1–16.1 hh)

Origin & Distribution

It is thought the breed can be traced back to the Normans who crossed their horses with native Irish ponies in the eleventh century. It is now distributed around the world.

Ireland

EXMOOR
GELDING

The Exmoor pony is unique in that it has remained unchanged since before Roman times. Looking at the Exmoor pony is like taking a step back some 2,000 years and seeing the ponies that existed at that time. The wild and solitary nature of Exmoor, a high moorland in north-east Devon, UK, where this pony still runs free, has led to this being the UK's oldest pure breed.

Features

Hardy to a legendary scale, the Exmoor is uniform with its 'toad' eyes (fleshy hood and pale colouration outlining the eye) and 'mealy' coloured muzzle. It is bay, brown or dun with black 'points' (legs) and must not have any white markings anywhere. Short legged and surefooted, this pony's size belies its strength.

Uses

Used by farmers and shepherds on Exmoor, it was also ridden to hunt the red deer that roamed there. Today its strength and strong personality are valued as a pony for adults and children and in harness. It's a good jumper with incredible stamina, making it ideal for trail riding and it is popular in the show ring.

Related Breeds

Kept pure by its remoteness, related breeds are really those genetic ones common to northern European pony breeds. Some similarities can be seen in the Dartmoor and New Forest, and it may be related to the Icelandic pony.

Size

Stallion ....119–129 cm
(11.3–12.3 hh)
Mare ....116.8–127 cm
(11.2–12.2hh)

Origin & Distribution

The Exmoor is thought to have arrived with the pre-Roman Celtic settlers although some believe it dates back to the Bronze Age. It's now found throughout the UK and in mainland Europe, North America and Scandinavia.

England

IRISH SPORT HORSE
GELDING

The increasing demand for sport horses in the 1980s, which encouraged the growth of warmblood horses, also resulted in the IRISH SPORT HORSE whose honesty, good conformation and stamina make it an ideal choice for horse sports. The iconic Irish Draught is the basis for this horse, and Ireland is renowned for producing these top-level competition horses.

Features

The breed combines the strength, endurance and powerful body of the Irish Draught with the speed and athleticism of the Thoroughbred. It can be any colour. The head is alert and attractive but may be slightly convex in appearance. Movement is straight, unexaggerated and free.

Uses

As the name suggests, this is a horse bred for competition at all levels including advanced. It has exceptional jumping ability, making it a great choice for eventing and show jumping. Still a popular choice as a hunter, its sense and stamina means it is often used by police forces, too. Strong enough to carry a substantial adult, it is popular with leisure riders.

Related Breeds

The Irish Draught, the Thoroughbred and the Connemara pony have all played their part in forming this great athlete.

Size

Stallion ....155–170 cm
(15.1–16.3 hh)
Mare ....155–170 cm
(15.1–16.3 hh)

Origin & Distribution

The Irish Sport Horse started as a cross bred horse but is now more commonly bred from horses who are themselves classified as an Irish Sport Horse. Due to its popularity for competition use, it is now found worldwide.

Ireland

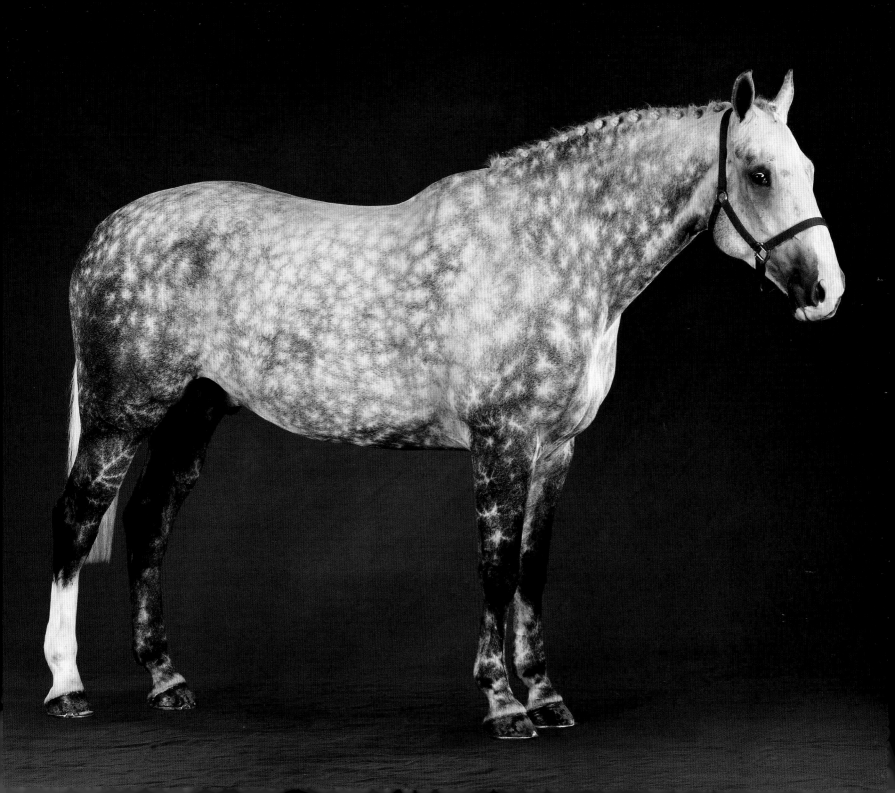

COMTOIS

MARE

The Comtois is a good-natured breed that is easy to train and still widely used in forestry to haul wood where access by vehicles is difficult. It is a very popular heavy horse breed in France, where it was bred in the Jura mountains on the border between France and Switzerland. Careful breeding today continues its success. Both Louis XIV and Napoleon used these horses for cavalry and artillery.

Features

The Comtois is a powerful, light draught horse with a deep girth, and a largish head with intelligent looking eyes and small ears. It has a stocky appearance with short, powerful legs with very little feather. Its coat is varying shades of chestnut darkening to bay with a thick mane and tail, which is often flaxen.

Uses

The Comtois is impressive for its performance in harness and, due to its limited range of colouring, it is also ideal for use working in matching pairs or teams. This breed is still used in woodland and vineyards but, due to its range of height, it is versatile enough to be ridden.

Related Breeds

In the nineteenth century, an improvement programme caused the Comtois to be bred with other draught horses such as the Percheron and Norman and in the early twentieth century, the Ardennais was also used in the breed.

Size

Stallion ....148–163 cm
(14.2–16 hh)
Mare ....148–163 cm
(14.2–16 hh)

Origin & Distribution

It's thought the original horses were brought to France from northern Germany in the 4th century. Today it has become popular outside France in the UK and the rest of Europe.

France

BRITISH SPOTTED
FILLY

A spotted coat pattern identifies the British Spotted pony, making it an eye-catching animal. It is also a quality pony, ranging from miniature to riding and cob types and it exemplifies real pony character. It's thought that in the distant past the spots may have acted as camouflage. Victorian paintings show spotted ponies were much valued as harness animals during this era.

Features

There are several coat patterns including leopard (shown opposite), few-spot leopard, blanket spotted, mottled pattern and snowflake (white spots on dark base coat). All spotted ponies must have some or all of the following: white sclera around the eye; mottled skin particularly around the lips, muzzle and ears; and striped hooves. It also has good substance and bone to complement its unique appearance.

Uses

In the show ring, the British Spotted pony stands out and has its own range of classes but it is a useful pony that can jump and take part in pony club activities, driving, trail riding, Western riding – in fact, it can turn its hoof to anything.

Related Breeds

Miniature horses can be found with a spotted coat. The Knabstrupper from Denmark and the Appaloosa are other spotted breeds, which may be related.

Size

Stallion ....82–148 cm
                  (8–14.2 hh)
Mare ....82–148 cm
                  (8–14.2 hh)

Origin & Distribution

Spotted ponies have been around for centuries and Edward I of England was recorded in 1298 as keeping a number of them. Today the British Spotted pony is found worldwide including the UK, mainland Europe, North America and Australia.

UK

CANADIAN BELGIAN

GELDING

This is a very big horse, with heights of over 193 cm (19 hh) not uncommon. Its huge size was developed in response to a need to develop a great heavy horse, which may have once been used to carry warriors in full armour. The CANADIAN BELGIAN is a very strong draught horse that can pull tremendous weights but is calm enough to work in a team, as a pair and even be ridden.

Features

They are always chestnut (also known as red roan or sorrel) in colour with flaxen manes and tails. Their head is comparatively small set on a thick and muscular neck above powerful shoulders. They have large hindquarters and their short, strong legs have a minimal amount of feathering.

Uses

Transported from their native Belgium to the USA and Canada in the late nineteenth century, this giant horse helped to build industry in these countries with their heavy hauling ability. Today they are resplendent in the show ring, matched in harness and also shown under saddle. They also compete in hand at shows.

Related Breeds

British breeds, Clydesdale and Shire have had crosses from the Belgian in the distant past.

Size

Stallion ....up to and over 193 cm
(19 hh)
Mare ....up to and over 193 cm
(19 hh)

Origin & Distribution

The Belgians' success in producing a super-strong, heavy horse led to its export to North America to produce this slightly lighter, longer legged version, the Canadian Belgian. This is the most numerous draught horse breed in North America.

Belgium

REPORTAGE

The partnership between humans and horses has certainly *gone the distance*. These behind-the-scenes pictures offer a snapshot of that relationship, with *perfectly-groomed* riders and horses performing at their best. PREPARE TO APPLAUD as they jockey for position and *go for gold.*

Equifest,
East of England
Showground,
Peterborough, UK

Best hoof forward
for both of us.

It's show time!

Focus, focus, focus.
No horseplay today!

Let's show
them how
it's done.

What do you think of today's cut and blow dry?

I'd keep it under my hat if I were you...

We'll give the big boys a run for their money!

We're all on our high horses today and going for red.

Check list:
Shampoo,
condition,
rinse,
detangle,
plait
- top to tail
grooming schedule.

Stop horsing around!

Get ready to go.

Nobody spends that much time on my tail

The behind-the-bins view of horse shows.

It's all in the styling lotion and plait action.

We're off to a flying start!

a jumping masterclass in action...

Victory! What a team!

Spot my nicely oiled hooves as we sail over.

Go easy with the hoof pick.
You said this was a pedicure!

Can I have some tips straight from the horse's mouth?

The look of unbridled love.

We definitely win on the sweet stakes!

Enjoying the tail end of the show.

Strictly Come
Prancing class,
anyone?

That looks more like
dancing to me.

The tension mounts...
who's getting
the big one?

That's going straight
on the stable door!

May the best horse win!
Another wonderful day
at Equifest.

GLOSSARY

Breed standard criteria agreed by breed clubs for a particular breed – the ideal horse or pony according to each country's specification

Colt an entire or un-castrated male horse usually under the age of four years

Cold blooded a term used to describe draught horses and some breeds of pony suitable for slow and heavy work

Conformation how the horse is proportioned – ideals are set out in each breed standard

Draught horse a heavy breed of horse developed to pull large weights, such as for pulling carts or ploughs. See Heavy horse

Evening performance finalists are judged under lights at night. Competitors often have top hats and evening dress and horses and ponies may wear sparkly glitter. Music is often played

Feathers some horse breeds have long hair on the back of their legs. This can vary from beginning behind the knee and covering the hoof, to a small amount lower down the leg at the back of the fetlock

Filly a young female horse usually under the age of four years

Gaits the four standard gaits of the horse are walk, trot, canter and gallop

Gelding a castrated male horse of any age. They are not usually gelded before six months of age

Hands (hh) a unit used to measure the height of horses and ponies, measured from the withers. One hand is equal to four inches

Heavy horse a large horse breed developed initially to carry fully armoured knights into battle, but later used for farm and draught work.

Hot blooded a term used to describe Thoroughbred and Arab horses – associated with their speed and endurance

In-hand a show class in which the animal is led either in a halter or in a bridle but is not ridden

Judge a person with experience chosen by a breed club or society to evaluate horses and ponies against their breed standards or class requirements

Knee action describes the horse bringing its knees up high towards its chin

Native breed a horse or pony breed that is native to a particular country, such as the Norwegian Fjord or the Welsh pony

Premium special award, usually including money, awarded to a breeding animal for excellence in order to encourage breeding from it

Qualifiers classes geared towards a particular championship at a particular show

Quality a term used widely when judging horses, normally taken to mean that the horse shows evidence of Thoroughbred influence in its head and, to an extent, in its body

Rare breed a horse or pony that meets the criteria of a country's rare breed society in its low numbers of breeding mares. Can be subdivided into categories such as critical, endangered, vulnerable, at risk and minority status

Ridden class a show class in which the horse is shown with a rider, usually performing all gaits

Rosette given to show winners and usually a different colour for each placing – red for first in UK and blue for first in USA

Scope the ability of the horse to perform its chosen job. For example, if it is has a lot of scope in jumping it is very capable

Show hunter a type or class of horse that would be suitable for hunting

Stallion parade often non-competitive, a parade of top class stallions held within a show for mare owners to evaluate them for possible breeding. Sometimes premiums are awarded

Stripped when the saddle is removed from a horse in the ridden class and the animal is led in-hand for the judge to evaluate its conformation

Warmblood a horse that is the product of a cross between a hot blood, such as a Thoroughbred, and a cold blood such as a draught horse. Often bred for carriage driving, riding and more recently competition

Working hunter a show class that includes jumping a round of rustic fences as part of the judging process

SHOWS

BRITAIN

Shows were once confined to summer but are now held all year round with winter and summer championships. They range from local club shows to championship level and many big shows have qualifying classes. Classes for a wide range of horse and pony breeds are also usually included in general agricultural shows.

March/April: British Show Pony Society; National Pony Society; Ponies UK Winter Championships; Shire Horse Society Show

May: Royal Windsor Horse Show

June: South of England Show; Three Counties Show; Cheshire County Show; Royal Highland Show; Royal Norfolk Show (all agricultural shows)

July: Great Yorkshire; Royal Welsh agricultural shows; Royal International Horse Show; Arab Horse National Show

August: Equifest, Peterborough; National Pony Society Summer Championship Show; Ponies UK Summer Championship Show; British Show Pony Society Summer Championship Show; British Skewbald and Piebald Association World of Colour Championships

September: Royal London Horse Show; National Hunter Supreme Championship Show; Royal County of Berkshire Show

October: Welsh National Foal Show; Horse of the Year Show, Birmingham

November: Royal Welsh Winter Agricultural Show

December: Olympia; London International Horse Show

IRELAND
August: Dublin Horse Show

AUSTRALIA
Major shows
Royal Adelaide Show; Royal Melbourne Show; Perth Royal Show; Royal Launceston Show; Royal Hobart Show

USA
Major shows:
The Kentucky State Fair World Championship Horse Show; Scottsdale Arabian Horse Show; The Grand National & World Championship Morgan Show; The US National Arabian & Half-Arabian Championship; Arabian & Half-Arabian Youth National Championship; Lexington Junior League; American Royal National Championship; All American Horse Classic; Hampton Classic; Devon Horse Shows

CANADA
Can-Am All Breeds Emporium; Royal Winter Fair; Canadian National Arabian Championship

CONTINENTAL EUROPE
Lausanne; Herning (Denmark); Wiesbaden; Aachen; Young Horse Championships Warendorf; Neumunster; Dortmund – all Germany; Hertogenbosch (Holland); Malmo; Gothenburg; (Sweden) Fontainebleau (France)

ASSOCIATIONS

BRITAIN
British Equestrian Federation
Stoneleigh Park, Kenilworth, Warwickshire
CV8 2RH
Telephone 02476 698871
Website www.bef.co.uk
Email info@bef.co.uk

British Show Pony Society
124 Green End Road, Sawtry, Huntingdon,
Cambs PE28 5XS
Telephone 01487 831376
Website www.bsps.com
Email info@bsps.com

British Skewbald and Piebald Association
Stanley House, Silt Drove, Tipps End, Welney,
Cambs PE14 9SL
Website www.bspaonline.com
Email bspashows@aol.com

The British Show Horse Association
Suite 16, Intech House, 34-35 The Cam Centre,
Wilbury Way, Hitchin, Herts SG4 0TW
Telephone 01462 437770
Website www.britishshowhorse.org
Email admin@britishshowhorse.org

Equifest
East of England Agricultural Society, East of
England Showground, Peterborough, Cambs
PE2 6XE
Telephone 01733 234451
Website www.equifest.org.uk

The National Pony Society
Willingdon House, 7 The Windmills, St Mary's
Close, Turk Street, Alton, Hants GU34 1EF
Telephone 01420 88333
Website www.nationalponysociety.org.uk
Email secretary@nationalponysociety.org.uk

Ponies (UK)
Chesham House, 56 Green End Road, Sawtry,
Huntingdon, Cambs PE28 5UY
Telephone 01487 830278
Website www.poniesuk.org
Email info@poniesuk.org

Sport Horse Breeding of Great Britain
96 High Street, Edenbridge, Kent, TN8 5AR
Telephone 01732 866277
Website www.sporthorsegb.co.uk
Email office@sporthorsegb.co.uk

USA
United States Equestrian Federation, Inc.
4047 Iron Works Parkway, Lexington, KY 40511
Telephone (859) 258 2472
Website www.usef.org

National Show Horse Registry
P.O. BOX 862, Lewisburg OH 45338
Telephone (937) 962 4336
Website www.nshregistry.org

CANADA
Equine Canada
2685 Queensview Drive, Suite 100, Ottawa,
Ontario, K2B 8K2
Telephone (613) 248 3433
Website www.equinecanada.ca
Email inquiries@equinecanada.ca

AUSTRALIA
Equestrian Australia
PO Box 673, Sydney Markets, NSW 2129
Telephone (61) 2 8762 7777
Website www.equestrian.org.au
Email info@equestrian.org.au

CONTINENTAL EUROPE
European Equestrian Federation (EEF)
Av. Houba de Strooper, 156 1020,
Brussels, Belgium
Telephone (351) 968 082 317
Website www.euroequestrian.eu
Email info@euroequestrian.eu

European Horse Network
Sweden
Telephone 46 (0) 8 627 21 85
Website www.europeanhorsenetwork.eu
Email info@europeanhorsenetwork.eu

Fédération Equestre Internationale
HM King Hussein I Building, Chemin de la
Joliette, 8 1006, Lausanne, Switzerland
Telephone (41) 21 310 47 47
Website www.fei.org

REFERENCES

British Native Ponies, Daphne Machin Goodall,
Country Life, 1962

The Handbook of Showing, Glenda Spooner,
London Museum Press, 1968

A History of British Native Ponies, Anthony Dent
and Daphne Machin Goodall, J. A. Allen, 1988

*Leading the Field: British Native Breeds of Horses
and Ponies*, Elwyn Hartley Edwards, Stanley
Paul, 1992

The Life, History and Magic of the Horse, Donald
Braider, Grosset and Dunlap, New York, 1973

Ponies in the Wild, Elaine Gill, Whittet Books,
1994

Shetland Breeds, Linklater, Alderson, et al,
Posterity Press USA, 2003

The World's Finest Horses and Ponies, edited by
Col Sir Richard Glyn, Harrap, 1971

AUTHOR'S ACKNOWLEDGEMENTS

I'd like to dedicate *Beautiful Horses* to the late
Glenda Spooner whose work with native ponies
inspired me always, and to Zara, an enthusiastic
Arab mare – without the need to pay for her
keep, I would never have become a writer. Also
to Odin, the Exmoor stallion, for giving me so
much success and pleasure in the show ring.

And always to Mick and Buffy.

PUBLISHER'S ACKNOWLEDGEMENTS

We would like to thank the following for their
help and cooperation in arranging the photoshoot:
Betsy Branyan, Jacqueline Hill and Emily Owen.

We would like to thank all of the horse owners
and breeders who allowed us to photograph their
horses and ponies:

American Quarter Horse **Caroline Hazell**
Appaloosa **Ami Dines**
Arabian **Clair Cryer**
British Riding Pony **Jenna Tate**
British Spotted **Carolyn Furnel**
British Warmblood **Natalie Arnold**
Canadian Belgian **David Mouland**
Cleveland Bay **Pamela Shipley**
Clydesdale **Andrew Fryer**
Coloured Cob **Rebecca Williamson**
Comtois **Emma Bailey**
Connemara **Laura Sheffield**
Dales **Denise Macleod**
Dartmoor **Tania Mizzi**
Exmoor **Annette Perry**
First Ridden Riding Pony **Simone Yule**
Friesian **Sam Willimont**
Haflinger **Sarah Hodges**
Hanoverian **Ginny Rusher**
Highland **Jane Murray**
Irish Draught **Katie Garrity**
Irish Sport Horse **Cerys Ford**
Lightweight Cob **Sam Cook**
Miniature Horse **Kerry Boon**
Morgan **Mrs T Reeve**
Native Coloured **Pat Hart**
New Forest **Jane Walker**
Norwegian Fjord **Jade Ward**
Rescue Horse **Mrs S.J. Wilson**
Riding Horse **Sofia Scott**
Shetland (chestnut) **Victoria Wakefield**
Shetland (two colour) **Claire Thompson**
Shire **Jodie Locke**
Suffolk **Glen Cass**
Thoroughbred **Donna Bamonte**
Traditional Coloured Cob **Colin Deane**
Welsh Cob/Welsh Section D (bay)
Georgina Wilkes
Welsh Cob/Welsh Section D (buckskin)
Richard Albon
Welsh Mountain Pony/Welsh Section A
Carol Simmons
Welsh Pony/Welsh Section B **Gareth Roberts**

INDEX